ATTRACTING
AN ANGEL

How to Get Money From Business Angels
and
Why Most Entrepreneurs Don't

Joseph A. Bockerstette
Martin C. Zwilling

Attracting an Angel

Introduction

As startup advisors and Angel investors, we consider funding at least a hundred new startups each year. When evaluating these opportunities, we see many of the same mistakes and we get asked many of the same questions.

- What is a Business Angel?
- What can I expect from an Angel?
- How can I get Angel funding?
- How do Angels value my Company?

This book addresses these questions and many more. It is written in a direct and simple style, and can be read cover-to-cover in an evening, making it easy to obtain the most useful information quickly.

Getting your startup funded by someone other than friends and family is very difficult. Through this book, we believe we're providing the insider information that will improve your odds of success.

Best Wishes,

Joe Bockerstette
Martin Zwilling

Chapter 1: Finding Your Angel

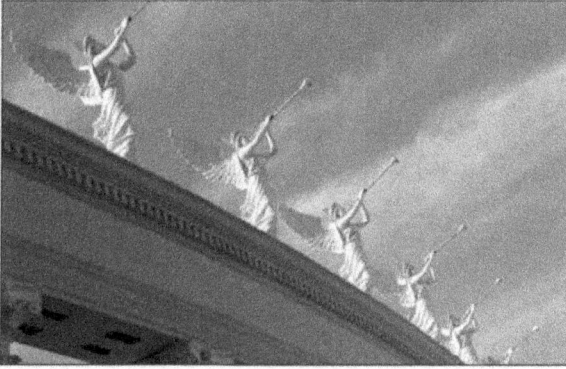

Angel Investors
are the **Dream** of
Every Entrepreneur

What makes a good Angel?

Fundraising is brutal. Actually, according to Paul Graham of Y Combinator fame, "Raising money is the second hardest part of starting a startup. The hardest part is making something people want." More startups may fail for that reason, but a close second is the difficulty of raising money.

According to Wikipedia, Angel investors in 2010 accounted for over $20 billion funneled into over 60,000 startups, or almost as much as all venture capital funds combined in the same year, but touching more than 60 times as many entrepreneurs. That's a lot of money from over 250,000 active Angels to a lot of startups, but according to Gust, one of the most popular websites for finding Angels, it's still true that over 90% of entrepreneurs who seek funding don't find an Angel.

Angel investors, by definition, are regular people, most often successful or retired entrepreneurs, who invest their own money in early-stage startups for a share of the equity. To be accredited, they must first certify to the SEC, under Section 413(a) of the Dodd-Frank Act, that they have an individual or joint net worth with their spouse exceeding $1,000,000, excluding the value of the their primary residence. That's just to make sure they have the means to support a set of wings.

On the business side, these people are typically focused on the investment areas they know well, and which they believe have a large opportunity for growth. As a rule of thumb, they look for startups that see the same large opportunity, with revenue projections of $20M or more within five years, and a high return (target is 10 times their investment), that can be realized via an exit in the same timeframe.

So the good Angels for you are ones with motives that are consistent with your values and an appreciation for your business opportunity perspective. This means they usually invest in people who have the right "chemistry", and areas of business they already know. They also tend to work locally, so they can "touch and feel" their investments.

Of course, the best Angels are active ones, meaning they are ready to write a check for the right business opportunity. Now it's time for you as an entrepreneur to do your own due diligence on them. Here are some questions you might ask as part of your own analysis, to find the right Angel for your requirements:

- How many investments have you made recently as an Angel?
- What is the typical investment size that you would consider?
- Do you normally invest alone, or syndicate with other Angels?
- Do you invest in seed startup companies, or prefer later stage ventures?
- Is your focus on a specific industry or geography, or more generic?
- What are your expectations on return rates and timeframes?

- What level of involvement do you normally expect to take with startups using your investment?

Even if you follow this recipe to find good Angels, you are likely to find that fundraising is a brutal challenge. But, if it results in an investor or two contributing and watching over your startup, you will definitely be one step closer to heaven.

What makes a good Angel group?

An Angel group is simply a flock of generally like-minded Angels, with more structure and organization to make them a bit easier to find and approach than individual Angel investors. The down side of approaching an Angel group is that they normally have an application, filtering, and due diligence process that will likely three months or more from your application until investor checks are written.

So if you are one of "the best of the best" entrepreneurs and have dozens of world-class investors and venture funds throwing money at you, there certainly is no need to go through the lengthier process of working with an organized Angel group. This means you could, in theory, get introduced by a friend to an Angel at a cocktail party, give him/her a three minute elevator pitch, and walk away with a check for your full amount on the spot.

For the rest of us, Angel groups can provide a viable and even preferred option for startup funding. For normal startups led by typical entrepreneurs, it is critical that you shake every tree, and explore every avenue, that might lead to the investment that you need to bring your company to the next level, with the confidence that your own due diligence on each member might be bypassed, due to the reputation and integrity of the group.

According to David S. Rose, often described as the Father of Angel Investing in New York, CEO of Gust (previously known as AngelSoft), and a serial entrepreneur, Angel groups over the past decade have become very structured and organized, with a professional trade association (the Angel Capital Association, founded by the Kauffman Foundation), standardized best practices, extensive syndication, a global web-based investment management platform, and a generally strong track record. According to the latest Halo Report in 2011 from the Angel Resource Institute (ARI), the median Angel group round is growing yearly, and is now up to $700,000, an increase of 40% over 2010.

In working with an Angel group, however, it's important to understand what makes it different (not better or worse, just different), from individual Angels on the one hand, and professional venture funds on the other. The biggest problem with individuals is that there are very few ways to easily find them or reach them, usually only by a personal introduction from someone who knows both of you. Their SEC registration status and contact information isn't listed on any public forum, so you can't send them email blasts, even if you want to.

Venture funds, on the other end of the spectrum, are highly visible, listed on the Internet, and in every phone book. Thus they have every entrepreneur in the country vying to get in front of them for funding. As a result, the major VC funds each receive between 5,000 and 10,000 funding requests a year. That means the odds of your over-the-transom business plan or pitch actually being read by them is near zero.

Angel groups, therefore, are right about in the middle between individual Angels and venture funds. Unlike individual Angels, they make themselves available to entrepreneurs (including having a website, soliciting funding applications even if you don't know someone there, running events, etc.), but unlike venture funds they typically receive hundreds of applications a year, instead of thousands. This is one of the reasons why the odds are about 10 times better for Angel funding than VC funding.

That being said, Angel groups don't have the budgets or staffs that venture funds do. Instead, they're composed of 25-100 individual people (many of them former entrepreneurs themselves), who volunteer their own time and effort to work together on funding startups. They have to coordinate a gaggle of Type-A personalities, while organizing (and personally funding) a process that will let them review hundreds of opportunities each year, so they can fund typically 5-10 of them.

In practice, Angel groups work on a monthly or quarterly cycle, beginning by reviewing all the submissions that have come in during the previous period, and selecting 5-15 of them for screening.

Those companies, who usually will not have had a previous relationship with anyone in the group, get to meet in person with a screening committee of 2-20 Angels, who will usually spend at least half an hour hearing the company's pitch. Thus the percentage of companies who manage to get in front of real investors for a real pitch through this method is very much higher than it is for either individual Angels or venture funds.

The screening committee will then invite 3-5 companies to return a few weeks later to present their pitch formally to the whole group, usually in a 15-30 minute session plus Q&A. During that meeting, dozens of legitimate, accredited investors will listen to the company's presentation, hoping to find interesting companies in which they can invest. Remember, unlike VCs, who do this as a job, Angel group members are voluntarily spending their time and their money because they really do want to invest in startups. No one does this just for 'fun' with no intention of investing.

If enough of the Angels in attendance are interested in hearing more about the company, there will usually be a series of follow-up meetings and due diligence sessions, resulting (everyone hopes) in either a term sheet for an investment (if the company doesn't already have one outstanding, and the group can corral enough members to come up with a reasonable total investment amount), or else in one or more Angels agreeing to invest alongside other investors the company has previously found.

Angel groups are not particularly proud of the length of time this process takes (these days it may be three months or more from submission to funding). The good news is that the groups, as an industry, are continually trying to reduce the length and complexity of this process. The Angel Capital Association (ACA) holds annual summits, training sessions and leadership conferences for its members, and many groups now routinely work together to syndicate investments that are larger than a single group has the resources to fund.

Finally, the development of Angel group platforms, such as Gust, means that much of the administrative burden is being lightened for entrepreneurs. You can now create a single investor relations web site for your company at no cost, and then simply share that with any Angel group you think might be a good match for you (both in the US and internationally). Each group's screening committee will review that site and use it as the basis for their internal collaboration as you move through their process.

So, the bottom line on all this is that organized Angel groups are far from perfect, but they are completely legitimate sources of startup funding, accounting for well over $100 million annually in seed funding. The major groups typically see many of even the hot deals in their area, but one of their main advantages is that they are often the best source to approach for getting a completely unbiased hearing for entrepreneurs who may not be quite as 'connected'.

Overall, the best Angel groups are led by executives who "have been there and done that," meaning they are experienced as investors as well as entrepreneurs. These executives tend to lead the individual Angels by example, and thus often initiate investments in startups that other members are quick to follow. So if you are looking for good Angel groups, find ones that have done the most investments, and led the most startups to success.

What to expect in an Angel investment?

Don't expect an Angel investor to listen to your pitch, quickly hand you a check, and then just disappear until you have a big return payment for him five years later. A key part of the motivation for most Angel investors is to provide mentoring and assistance, based on their own experience, so they usually expect to be put on your Board of Directors, for monthly updates and active involvement in key decisions.

Also, they will expect a chunk of equity ownership in your company, typically between 20% and 40%, commensurate with the size of their investment compared to the current valuation of your startup. They are looking for a rate of return on their investment, over the years of waiting, of up to 10 times their initial investment. This return expectation may seem high, but when tempered with the knowledge that the risk in unsecured and high, it becomes more reasonable.

Some want securities - either common stock or preferred stock with certain rights and liquidation preferences over common stock. Some even ask for convertible debt, or redeemable preferred stock, which provides a clearer exit strategy for the investor. Some Angels ask for the right of first refusal to participate in the next round of financing. While this sounds eminently reasonable, more venture capitalists will want their own players only, or certain investment minimums, so this strategy has the potential to limit whom future participants might be.

In order to protect their investment, Angels often ask the business to agree to not take certain actions without their approval. These actions can include a vote on selling all or substantially all of the company's assets, issuing additional stock to existing management, selling stock below prices paid by the investors or creating classes of stock with liquidation preferences or other rights senior to the Angels' class of security. Angels may also ask for price protection, that is, anti-dilution provisions that will result in their receiving more stock should the business issue stock at a lower price than that paid by the Angels.

The net outcome is that working with Angel investors is not simple or cheap. Their money, as well as their expertise, can be very beneficial, but you as the entrepreneur are no longer in absolute control. Communication on a regular basis is critical, and usually there are milestones and timelines to be met. If you want complete and autonomous control, you should consider "bootstrapping" with organic growth, which means funding your own business.

What are the trends in Angel investing?

If you are new to the entrepreneurial world of startups, you are likely confused by the terminology of seed-stage, lean startups, micro-VCs, and Super Angels. Don't be embarrassed, since even professional investors are often confused these days by the new terms, as well as old terms used with new meanings.

Here is just a sampling of the latest terminology and trends from investor literature and the Internet, that every entrepreneur should know who may be looking for funding now, or down the road:

- **Early-stage startup.** Every startup is early-stage to someone. For a startup Founder, this stage is when the "big idea" has become a passion for him, but he hasn't written anything down yet. For Angel investors, early-stage means there is a good business plan and maybe a prototype, and only a small amount of customer revenue. For VCs, early-stage may mean customer revenue is less than $10 million. Thus the more precise term these days for very early pre-revenue startups is "seed stage."

- **Micro-VCs.** These are an emerging group of professional investors (venture capitalists, etc.), who are investing from a fund of other people's money, with a particular focus on seed-stage startup opportunities. Usually the investment amounts are small, and meant to cover a large number of entrepreneurs.

- **Super Angels.** These are the Angel counterparts to traditional VCs, who previously only invested their own money, but now have begun raising funds from outside investors to do more deals per year. Like most Angels and micro-VCs, however, they still start with relatively small sums of money, often investing only $10,000 to $50,000 in the first increment.

- **Series-seed round**. Since the economic downturn started, neither Angels nor VCs have given much attention to startups without a product and a revenue stream. That has been left to the realm of friends and family. In the last couple of years, there has been a resurgence of interest, some say a bubble, by both Angels and VCs, in a pre-Series-A kicker to identify promising startups with seed funding, before major equity has been given away.

- **Business accelerator.** This term is replacing "startup incubator," which is a facility provided by an individual, university, or local community for any new startups to congregate for almost no cost, with the hope of learning from each other. The top business accelerator models are Y Combinator and TechStars, who select only the best applicants, have a demanding process, provide experienced coaching/ mentoring, some seed funding, and a required exit in about six months. Incremental investment likely follows for the best graduates.

- **Lean startup.** This is a concept coined (and trademarked) by Eric Ries a couple of years ago, primarily for software and web application startups. Lean startups operate on minimal money, an open source environment, and assume multiple iterations, with customer feedback, to get it right. A popular phrase heard in this environment is "rinse and repeat." Today, if you do well in this mode, you will get funded if and when you need it.

Overall, the biggest issue for early-stage startups still is funding – how much should you expect, who provides it, and how much of your future company should you give up to get it? The trend for investors, including micro-VCs and Super Angels, is to place "lots of little bets," ($10K to $50K) with milestones applied, which can then lead to incremental and larger funding checks.

Pundits call this the "spray and pray" approach to funding. Even though significant deal vetting and filtering is performed by the investor teams running these seed programs, in effect, they spray little bits of capital onto as many good ideas as possible, help them along, and pray some eventually strike it big.

Despite these pundits, we sense a fundamental change in the early-stage financing eco-system. With the Internet and other powerful but inexpensive business tools, the cost of development and rollout of new startups is lower than ever before, so the "big bang" theory of funding no longer makes sense. This should be a wake-up call for traditional entrepreneurs and investors alike.

Another hot new approach now seen around the country for assisting startups looking for funding has been "crowd-sourcing" sites (Kickstarter) or "crowd-pitching" events (Funding Universe). These are variations on a "crowd-funding" theme to raise money for a startup through social networks and voting at public events. We're still waiting for a startup to proclaim real success from this approach.

Crowd-sourcing tools, usually Internet applications, use the social media to poll for interest, feedback, and ultimately some funding for the startup. This is a complex task, especially as it involves creating an accurate yet compelling offer, collecting the money, and rewarding the investors.

Crowd-pitching is an offline event, but logically similar, which gives several candidates an opportunity to pitch to a crowd of interested people for a couple of minutes, after which the crowd "votes" with some play-money to pick the best candidate, who then wins some nominal investment amount or services.

On April 5, 2012, President Obama signed into law the Jumpstart Our Business Startups Act (JOBS). According to Wikipedia, "it is intended to encourage funding of United States small businesses by easing regulations." Basically, the bill seeks to remove or reduce the SEC accreditation requirements now put on Angel investors, and the SEC registration requirements for companies selling securities.

The JOBS Act specifically authorizes crowd-funding. It lifts some of the SEC's traditional prohibitions and requirements, and allows a company to sell securities via crowd-funding sites and/or social networking sites so long as the company (and its intermediary, if applicable) complies with the following key restrictions:

- The company may only raise a maximum of $1 million (or $2 million if the company provides potential investors with audited financial statements);

- Each investor is limited to investing an amount equal to the lesser of (i) $10,000 or (ii) 10% of his or her annual income.

The issuer or the intermediary, if applicable, must take a number of steps to limit the risk to investors, including (i) warning them of the speculative nature of the investment and the limitations on resale, (ii) requiring them to answer questions demonstrating their understanding of the risks, and (iii) providing notice to the SEC of the offering, including certain prescribed information.

Many investment experts are concerned that crowd-funding could lead to more fraud and scams by phantom companies, and severe disappointment to untrained investors who see no return for many years. Time will tell on this one.

Are Angels really venture capitalists?

An Angel investor is not a venture capitalist, since he or she is investing his or her own money. Venture capitalists (VCs), or institutional investors, are paid to invest other people's money, and measured on the rate of return they get. Venture capital funds are commercial organizations whose business it is to find the 5-20 companies each year that they believe have a chance of being one of the only 80 companies a year that will ultimately exit in a sale of over $50 million.

Overall, VCs are looking for big numbers, in relation to Angels or other potential investors. They are looking for products (generally not services) that will be "must haves" for customers, not "nice to haves," and they are looking to multiply their money by at least ten times in five years.

That means the target market must be large (at least $1 billion), proven and growing, with revenue potential of at least $50 million within five years. Initial investment targets are usually larger than $2 million, sometimes up to $25 million or $50 million. To make this work, you will need an initial valuation of at least $5 million.

Venture capitalists (VCs), in general, are not looking for business from first-time startups. Sure, there is always some seed funding (10% of overall deal flow), but you can bet that this money goes to entrepreneurs who have been there before and won. Angels are also moving up-stage (meaning larger investment into more mature opportunities), leaving a bigger and bigger black hole for new startups. Your friends and family are really the only answer until you have a significant revenue stream.

Back to VCs, Silicon Valley venture capital firms are still the most active. In fact, most of the most active investment firms are located there, although NY now has moved solidly into second place (ahead of Boston). That doesn't mean that you have to live in one of these places to be considered, but it helps.

The unfortunate (but true) situation is that the vast majority of startups that do receive venture capital funding were originally referred-to the VC by someone in their network, such as a current or former portfolio CEO. So what can you do to get to the head of the venture capital investment queue?

As with any potential investor situation, the first requirement is to create an investment-grade business plan. This means build a plan that hits all the hot buttons; problem/solution, executive team, competition, business model, reasonable financial projections, and what's in it for the investor. Be ready with a **killer** executive summary, investor presentation, and financial model.

Another important requirement for VCs is to line up a winning team. You have probably heard this before, but investors look harder at the people than they do the idea (bet on the jockey rather than the horse). They want Founders who have been there and done that, in the same business domain. Both operating executives and top advisors count.

As with Angels, timing is critical. Remember you only have one chance for a good first impression. Don't try to talk your way to a deal before you have the documentation. Practice every step, including the elevator pitch to get the first meeting. Use friends, family, and Angels, if possible, to get a product shipped, revenue, and customers first before the VC connection.

The next step is to identify the right people in the right firms. Mass mailing your business plan to every VC in the book won't get you any credibility or traction. Investment firms specialize by business sectors, and each partner within the firm has a specialty. If you are in "energy," do your homework to build a list of the top players in this segment.

If possible, make a personal connection, directly or indirectly. If you don't personally know anyone on this list, talk to every professional friend you have to see who they know. Get introduced via one of the social networks, or a professional organization, before you approach a VC with a business proposal.

Current market conditions should convince you to be totally thorough, thoughtful and aggressive in your approach and presentations. But now is the time to work all the investor alternatives, and remember to work friends, family, and Angels before you tackle the big boys.

What makes you attractive to Angels?

In fact, being touched by an Angel can lead you to your dreams of a new and successful business, but it doesn't happen without planning, hard work, and careful preparation. Most Angel investors are seeking psychic as well as financial benefit from their investment. Do your homework first to get their attention, but don't expect anyone to swoop down and wave a magic wand.

So what should you do to prepare for this stage in your venture, and optimize your chances of making it through the process? Let's talk about some of the most important action items to best prepare you for success in achieving a funding event with Angels.

First of all, don't hesitate to incorporate the business now. If you expect to require external funding, you should incorporate as an S-Corp, C-Corp, or LLC, rather than the more expeditious sole proprietorship or partnership. The corporate entity lends itself best to the concept of "sharing" equity required by investors, and unincorporated entities don't get funding.

It's also never too early to start lining up an experienced team. Remember the old adage that "investors fund people, not ideas." That's why this item is so important, and is probably the biggest stumbling block we see in getting through the initial Angel screening. If the Founders are not experienced, find a couple of advisors from the business sector to fill the gap.

On the business side, you need to get your Internet domain name and website to match your company name. In today's world, if you don't have a web site up and running, you will not be perceived as a real company. Investors routinely go to candidate web sites to get a feel for the tone and scope of the company, as well as its maturity and offerings. Reserve the company name on social networks to protect it.

Another step toward establishing real credibility is to define your intellectual property. File a patent and trademarks to show real intellectual property. Having a defensible competitive advantage or "barrier to entry" is another critical step to funding, and another common stumbling block during all phases of the funding process. Start early on this one, or you will lose the opportunity.

Of course, for a product company, it's important to build a prototype product early. A conundrum for many frustrated entrepreneurs is that they need money from investors to design and build a prototype product, yet most Angel investors expect to see at least a prototype before they invest. Use your own money or friends and family to demonstrate progress early.

Credibility on the business case side begins with an investor presentation and executive summary. Investors expect a one or two-page executive summary sheet for the initial screening, backed up by a ten-slide PowerPoint investor presentation. Remember to aim the content of both of these at investors, not customers. They must amplify your "elevator pitch" to investors, as well as key points from the business plan and the financial model.

Following the summary and presentation, professional investors expect an investment-grade business plan. Every entrepreneur needs a professional business plan for their own use, whether they intend to seek investor funding or not. As a Founder, you may think that everyone understands your vision and plan from your passion and words, but it doesn't work that way. It should answer every question an investor or associate might ask, including current valuation, funding needed, and exit strategy.

On the financial side, you need a financial model to buttress your projections, and allow alternatives to be quickly evaluated. Like the business plan, a financial model is required as much for your own use as to impress Angel investors. In most cases, a Microsoft Excel spreadsheet is adequate, with projection formulas for revenue, costs, and cash flow over the next five years. Variables for "what if" questions add credibility.

Another credibility step, if you can accomplish it, is to close at least one initial customer. This must be someone who is willing to pay real money for your product or service. Free trials don't count. All the conviction and market research in the world are no substitute for real customers paying real money. This is called "validating the business model."

As a final point, we always recommend that you network to the maximum with investor connections. The last and possibly most important action item is to build relationships with investors and friends of investors BEFORE you need their help in building your company. A good start is taking an active role in relevant technology groups, trade associations, university activities, and local business groups.

If you do get rejected the first time, don't give up, and don't expect a simple answer on your rejection reason from most Angels. They will probably tell you to come back later, after you have finished the product, signed up a few customers, or reached some other future milestone. This is called "not burning any bridges," in case you start to show traction and they want to come back into the deal.

How do you find Angels?

With today's access to the Internet, and Google searches, it really isn't that hard to find flocks of Angels. The first place to look is on the most popular Internet collaboration platforms for Angels, including Gust, GoBIGNetwork, and the Angel Capital Association (ACA).

Gust [www.gust.com] is one the most reliable sources of information on Angel investor groups across the world, and the software is used by most of the other Angel organizations mentioned below for deal flow. It boasts over 600 Angel groups, 150 Venture Capital organizations, 35,000 investors, and 125,000 entrepreneur and startup profiles.

As an entrepreneur, simply enter your location online, and it will list the Angel and VC organizations near you. You can then begin your application to one or more of these organizations right on the same screen.

The Keiretsu Forum [www.keiretsuforum.com] is another large portal, which claims to be the world's largest individual Angel investor network, with 850 accredited investor members throughout twenty one chapters on three continents. Since Keiretsu Forum's founding in

2000, its members have invested over $260M in technology, consumer products, healthcare/life sciences, and real estate companies. The founding chapter is in Silicon Valley, California. A caveat is that this is a for-profit organization, so fees to present may be significant.

On the East Coast, the New England Investment Network [newenglandinvestmentnetwork.com] is a series of website templates for matching Angel investors seeking investment opportunities with entrepreneurs seeking capital. The caveat here is that this network doesn't have a personal touch, as it only facilitates the exchange of contact information, so the matchmaking is left up to you. The reach is very broad, however, with 30 networks worldwide covering over 80 countries in Europe, North America, South America, Africa, Asia and Australasia, and over 200,000 members worldwide.

Another alternative is the Angel Capital Association [www.angelcapitalassociation.org] whose membership includes more than 160 Angel groups and 20 affiliate organizations from 44 US states and 6 Canadian provinces. These groups represent more than 7,000 Angels and are funding approximately 800 new companies each year and managing an ongoing portfolio of more than 5,000 companies throughout North America.

Actually numbers and locations are just the beginning. The challenge is to find the right Angel or Angel group for your startup, and help them find you. Once you know the location of Angels near you, the best strategy is to be proactive in getting to know them personally, and it's never too early to start.

For maximum credibility, you should start networking for potential investors to build relationships a few months before you start asking for money. As we often say, Angels invest in people, more often than they invest in ideas. That means they need to know you, or someone they trust who does know you (warm introduction).

They also favor entrepreneurs who are experienced in starting a company, and experienced in the business domain of the startup. Your business model may be very attractive, but if you are new to this game, you may not be fundable. In this case you need a partner who has deep domain knowledge and a track record of building businesses.

Of course, you need to remember that Angel investors are people too. Investors expect you to understand their motivation, respect their time, and show your integrity in all actions. They probably won't respond well to high pressure sales tactics, information overload, or bribes.

In fact, their preference is to get involved directly with you and your team. This means they are generally only interested in local opportunities. It won't help your case or your workload to do an email blast and follow-up with 60,000 investors around the world. If there is no one in your area interested or experienced in your type of business, you may have to move to Silicon Valley or Boston, or wherever the right Angels for your domain congregate.

A related issue is the size of the investment you need. Angel investors tend to limit the size of individual investments to $250K or less, and even in groups they rarely consider requests for more than one million dollars. If you need more, you need to focus on venture capital territory.

Of course, Angels are really mortals, so it never hurts to entice Angels to play along. They want to make a difference. Asking an Angel to work with your company in an advisory role is a great way to establish a relationship that may lead to a cash investment. If you impress the Angel, it will likely make her at least an Archangel (advocate) when it comes to funding.

Also, remember Angels beget Angels. That means that once you get the first one, he or she becomes your best advocate for finding more. Investment Angels don't like to travel alone, so they will bring in others if they can (it's called share the risk).

Finally, don't forget passive Angels. These are Angel investors who are private, meaning they don't go to meetings, but will invest if someone they trust brings them an attractive opportunity. Find the right investment advisor, or member of your advisory board, and the "match-making" will happen.

In all cases, a complete business plan is always required. Maybe friends and family will give you money with no plan, but Angel investors expect a real plan. All professional investors know that entrepreneurs who start a business without a written plan almost always fail.

Make sure your financial projections and opportunity are in the right ballpark. Investors won't fund people who don't push the limits, or inversely won't recognize business realities. Here are some rules of thumb. Your fifth-year revenue projections better be between $20M-

$100M. Smaller numbers mean a low return, and larger ones aren't usually credible

Another criteria for most Angel investors is that your business domain and your character must be squeaky clean and not failure prone. Certain business sectors have historical high failure rates and are routinely avoided by investors. These include food service, retail, consulting, work at home, and telemarketing. Also, don't expect investor enthusiasm for your gambling site, porn site, gaming, or debt collection business.

Our summary message is that the best Angel you can find, or might find you, is a local high net-worth individual, with whom you or your advisors have an established prior relationship.

Is there a dark side to Angel investing?

A few Angel investors have slipped or fallen from their lofty perch, so entrepreneurs must take great care to validate the character and reputation of every prospective investor, just like you would for every business partner or vendor. The entrepreneur's tendency to be in a huge hurry to obtain the funding can end up being disastrous, and play into the hands of a few less scrupulous investors.

Many entrepreneurs believe all money is created equal. As long as somebody recognizes their million-dollar idea and writes them a check, the source really doesn't matter. In fact, most Angels are pure, but there are some exceptions that may cost you more than an investment:

- **Shark Angels.** This is the ultimate bad guy whose sole intention of getting involved in early-stage investing is to take advantage of what they believe is the entrepreneur's lack of financial and deal-making experience. If the term sheet process turns to pure torture, it may be time to respectfully bow out.

- **Litigious Angels.** The litigious investor will look for almost any excuse to take you to court. This type of investor never really focuses on the returns your company can deliver, but instead tries to make money by intimidation, threats and lawsuits. They know you won't have the resources to fight them, so they count on you "caving." Keep your attorney close by your side.

- **Superior Angels.** A number of successful business people, some of whom become

Angels, develop the belief that they are destined for greatness because of their clear superiority over others. These are usually overbearing, negative people who are hypercritical of every decision you make. Don't be intimidated into bad decisions.

- **Control-freak Angels.** This Angel starts out looking like your new best friend. Once you are funded, he waits until you hit your first pothole and then points out "gotcha" clauses in your agreement that give him more control. This escalates into a requirement that he must step in to run your company himself. Only your Board can save you here.

- **Tutorial Angels.** The tutorial investor is not after control, but wants to hold your hand on every issue. The mentoring offer always sounds good up front. But after they write the check, it soon becomes apparent that their desire to be helpful 24 hours a day is a nuisance at best. Initially, your gratitude for their investment may prompt tolerance, but eventually the burden wears you down. Keeping your distance is the best solution.

- **Has-been Angels.** These tend to appear with every perturbation in the economy. They are usually high-flyers with a liquidity problem. They are still at the country club every day, but are now running up a tab. They will meet with you, and ask a thousand questions, but never get around to closing the deal. Learn to ask the closing questions.

- **Dumb Angels.** Wealth is not synonymous with business savvy. You can spot dumb Angels by the questions they ask (or don't ask). If they ask superficial questions or don't understand business, a successful long-term relationship is not likely. But don't forget that people with wealth usually may have some savvy friends to meet.

- **Brokers posing as Angels.** These people are all over the place, often posing as lawyers and accountants. They have little intent to invest in your company, and will eventually solicit you to sign a fee agreement to pay them to introduce you to actual investors. Brokers are often worth the fee, but don't be misled about who is the Angel.

- **Unqualified Angels.** These Angels can't really afford to be Angels. Any investment amount under consideration should be comfortable for the Angel investor. The Angel must see this class of investment as completely discretionary, where all of the money may be lost, but the experience will be one that the Angel benefits from and enjoys nonetheless. If the money invested is too important to the Angel, and he then stresses over the investment, the interests of the Angel and entrepreneur can easily grow at odds with one another.

How do you avoid most of these? Whenever possible, only accept investments from individuals in credible, professional Angel investing organizations - not people who solicit you. Even then, do your own due diligence in the business community. Ask what other companies they've invested in, and talk to the CEOs of those companies to find out what kind of investor they've been.

Also, make sure you use a standard term sheet from a reputable Angel group, or your lawyer writes the initial investment document or term sheet. Don't wait for the random investor to provide one, which may contain special clauses and fine print that can come back to bite you. This is not the time to blindly charge ahead.

Chapter 2: Planning Your Business

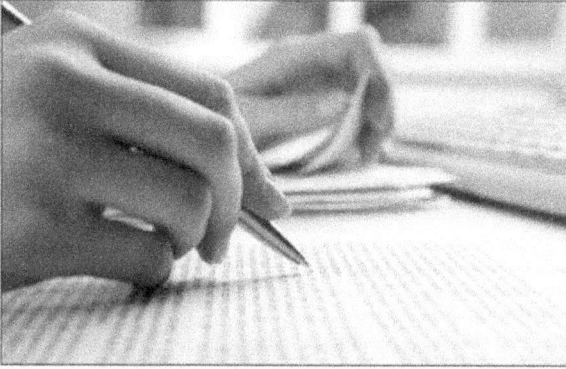

Every Entrepreneur
Needs a **Plan**

Why the Business Plan Matters

While entrepreneurs typically use the business plan to communicate their startup intentions to prospective investors, it's real usefulness lies in the careful thought and reasoning that is used by the management team to create the plan. What matters is not whether the plan is right (because plans are never really right) but the quality of thinking and effort that goes into its development. You should think of the plan as a means to an end. The end is what you want prospective Angels to know about your business. The means is the business you are designing from a blank sheet of paper. When reviewing a business plan, Angel investors evaluate the design of the startup business and the quality of the thinking that went into that design. The plan itself is merely the documented outcome of the design process.

The business plan also documents the living, breathing, unfolding story and roadmap of your startup intentions. The plan should generally be about 25 pages long, plus appendices, and cover a five-year time horizon. It should be treated as a continuous work-in-process that captures your latest thinking and incorporates your lessons learned along the way. Every experience and interaction provides an opportunity to improve the quality of the business design and your plan should reflect that progress. You never want to be caught saying, "Please excuse my business plan, it's out of date". Or "I need to update my business plan one of these days".

While a good business plan doesn't guarantee an Angel investment, a poor plan will most certainly cause the Angel to pass on the opportunity.

Describe your Business Purpose

Begin the business plan with a basic description of the business you are starting and its corporate form. You should give serious consideration at the start to what form the corporation will take as it may make a meaningful difference in investor interest. While some investors will only invest in C corporations, others may only invest in LLC's.

Tax considerations are also very important here. Many startups delay incorporation until the first formal round of financing, which is too late. At this point your entity may already have several million in valuation, so the IRS will tax your shares at that value immediately as income, just when your cash flow is at its lowest.

The solution again is to incorporate early and filing an "83(b) election" with the IRS within 30 days of the agreement. This directs the IRS to tax the stock at the time of the grant (when it usually is worth very little), minimizing potential tax liability. Then you will only have to pay tax on the increasing value of your shares when they are sold.

There are limitations to the number of investors allowed in certain corporations as well. Time spent with an attorney at startup can save headaches later on. We have seen many startups legally restructured upon receiving their initial investment.

It is helpful to summarize the stage of maturity of your business.

Have you….

- Developed a concept on paper only?
- Produced a prototype?
- Trialed products with customers?
- Generated revenue?
- Received prior investments?

What is the purpose of your startup? How did you get here? Angels want to know the background to your business. Tell them where your idea came from. Describe your journey to date and a brief history of the major milestones that have gotten you to where you are. Provide a good sense of the history and current status of the business and why an Angel investment is right for you at the present time.

Provide a brief description of where the business is going. Summarize the short-term plan and timeline (maybe 3 – 6 months out) to the next major milestone. Angels are particularly interested in the commercialization timing of your venture.

Develop your Value Proposition

The value proposition is a short statement that clearly identifies the target customer, the customer's problem and the pain that it causes, how your unique solution addresses this problem, and the net benefit of this solution from the customer's perspective.

All startups should be conceived with the development of a well thought-out and thoroughly understood value proposition. The value proposition provides the foundation on which a successful business can be built. It is often misunderstood and taken for granted, which results in wasted time, money and talent spent on a mission that leads to frustration and disappointment. While entrepreneurs freely toss around the term "value proposition," they rarely offer an insightful understanding of the "value" their business is providing and, more importantly, who their real customer is and what valuable benefit their customer receives.

A strong value proposition contains four very important statements.

- **Identifies the target customer.** While most entrepreneurs quote a large market size and the impressive dollars spent in that market, not many can specifically name who will buy their product or service, how many of these target customers exist and where they can be found.

  The target customer is the person or organization who will be motivated to purchase the product you are offering. This motivation comes from possessing the painful problem (to be discussed next) that your solution is intended to alleviate. It's not uncommon to see the customer misidentified by the entrepreneur; for example when the user is different from the party who approves the usage, who is different from the one who pays. In cases of confusion, think carefully about the acquisition process versus the payment process. The customer is generally the one with the authority to make the purchase. You should develop a target customer profile by writing a short paragraph or two describing common customer traits or characteristics for the person or entity whose problem you will be solving. To the extent possible, you should understand what makes this customer different and unique from the larger market population. Out of this exercise you should have a clear understanding of what makes them a "target" customer. If you haven't found a description that fully fits, then you don't yet know your value proposition. Keep defining until you really understand whose problem you will be solving and why that person is the obvious target. It's not uncommon that a startup has the ability to serve more than one target customer. If this is the case, develop a unique customer profile for each customer type.

- **The customer's problem and the pain it causes.** This statement gets at the basic level of desire a customer may have for the solution that you offer. Often the desire can be stated as a problem to be solved, such as an injury to be healed. Alternatively, the desire may be stated as a strong want of something, such as the need to have the coolest new Smartphone or automobile. Also important in this consideration is how satisfied the customer is with solutions that are already available. If the problem is being sufficiently solved today, the customer will have less desire to seek out a new solution. The stronger the pain or want exists, the more likely the customer will be open to your potential solution. Either way, a strong desire provides the necessary beginning of a winnable value proposition.

The problem statement should clearly articulate the customer's problem in everyday terms. What is the problem; why does it occur and how frequently; what is the underlying cause?

The problem statement should also describe the level of pain felt by the customer. A problem without pain is probably not worth solving, so you should know how important it is to the customer that their problem gets solved. This step is very often overlooked, as entrepreneurs frequently assume that the pain level that is much greater than actually exists for the customer. This hopeful thinking comes from a lack of study and the development of empirical evidence that defines the importance of the problem.

While the pain level can be expressed in dollars, what matters here is knowing the extent to which the target customer desires that the problem be solved relative to available options. The more painful the unsolved customer problem, the greater is the opportunity to find a place in the market.

- **How your unique solution addresses this problem.** Here you are addressing the core purpose of your new business. You must convince the investor that your solution is better than, unique from, and more highly desired by your target customer, than all other available options. What makes the solution compelling? What have you discovered that others in the market before you have missed? When its unique solution solves a customer's painful problem better than all other options, the startup has successfully cleared an important early hurdle to a successful venture.

- **The net benefit of this solution from the customer's perspective.** Here is where true potential is discovered. First, value is solely perceived in the eyes of the customer. If you see the solution as very valuable, but the target customer doesn't, then there is no business. What is it worth to the customer to solve their painful problem? Begin by thinking about the gross value of the customer's desire. It can be expressed in many ways, such as reducing waste, increasing revenues, restoring good health, saving time, improving skills, having fun, etc.

Second, the benefit of your solution should be weighed, initially against its cost, and secondly, compared to the other options available to the customer. While a customer may desire your solution, your cost could preclude them from purchasing it or alternatively another solution that isn't as good may be more affordable and therefore more attractive to the customer. Very few solutions are desired at any cost. Understanding your position in the customer's mind is a critical element when considering growth potential and the ultimate market opportunity.

A compelling value proposition may be a winner, but how does one know? The answer lies in validation. If you want to build a winner, get to know and understand your customer. Learn everything about their painful problem and why they must solve it. Know what they currently do to address the problem and how satisfied they are with that solution. Learn the real economics of the problem. How much does the problem cost the customer? Does it affect their quality of life? What are they willing to pay to solve it? Get credible customers on your company's side. Sponsor independent studies that validate your solution claims. To what extent do you have evidence to support your claims?

How can you convince investors that your value proposition is the big winner? Demonstrating that a paying customer exists with a painful problem that your solution solves better than any other makes for an excited investor conversation. Angels are drawn to strong value propositions with evidence that customers are willing to pay strong prices for considerable value.

Define your Products Portfolio

Describe your products, what makes them special, their commercialization readiness and the major product development plans facing the company. Why is your solution better than the alternatives? You should build a strong case for the superiority of your product portfolio versus the competitive options available to the customer. Angel investors do not want to guess at what you intend to sell to execute your value proposition.

Where appropriate, and especially if your company will be commercializing a product under development, offer a product strategy and map that summarizes your target product specification, the current development status, extended product vision, major milestones and projected timeline. Where new product development is central to your value proposition, Angels will be keenly interested in assessing your product direction.

Clearly articulate what you will be selling to generate revenues for your startup. Think of this as a price list that you will be giving to prospective customers. List products with brief descriptions, units of measure and selling prices and terms. Provide at least a rough cut of the timing of introduction for each product or group of products. Identify how products will be provided, the source for your products and the total product costs.

Address the competitive barriers to entry, particularly when they are formidable. Include the description and status of all intellectual property filings and their relevance in the barriers to entry discussion. A strong IP portfolio may be the startups' most valuable asset.

Project your Revenue Potential

Good business plans contain a market overview providing a larger context of revenue potential for the business. While this is an interesting and useful exercise, it is not enough to know that a market is really big. What is important, however, is to know exactly what customers will buy the product, how many of them exist in the intended geography and what their buying patterns will likely be once your product is available. Through this effort, you will be able to specifically project the full annual revenue potential for the business you intend to create. From this baseline, you can estimate the growth trends of your target customers, the percent of market share than you will capture over time and the overall growth rate of the business. It is much more powerful and believable to build your revenue model from the ground up.

Once you have established the revenue potential for the new business and your plan to capture your share of the market, you want to clearly describe how the business will make money. This is a critical element in the attractiveness of the startup. Angels want to know that the operating business will be large enough to pay back substantial returns on their early investment. This should include a thorough presentation of gross margins based on the best evidence from your experience.

Obtaining early customer involvement is a great way to sell your opportunity to Angels. As soon as practical, you should get a key customer on board trying out your solution and providing valuable feedback on its prospects. The more customer involvement you can demonstrate the more Angel interest you will attract. Know your customers. Know why they like your product best. Know what they are willing to pay for your product. Know why they resist changing to your product from an otherwise acceptable alternative. And know what customers other options are and how they compare to yours. Resist the temptation to underestimate competitions' offerings. Your customers will not make that same mistake.

Analyze the Broad Environment

You will need to provide an assessment of the broader trends affecting your startup. What is the larger industry and the specific niche the company will be competing in? Is the market moving in a direction favorable for the company's solution or is the market moving toward other options? What are the demand drivers affecting the revenue opportunity? What are the demographics of your target customer and how is that changing? What impact could the government have on your prospects? What approvals are needed to commercialize your product?

Provide a thorough review of the competition, what they currently provide the customer, how well they meet customer needs, their strengths and weaknesses and their size. Directly compare your product offering with competitor products, even if there are shortcomings. While providing this analysis, you want to estimate the total market you are addressing. Do not underestimate the competitive environment. There is always some level of competition.

Finally, provide a brief description of any business partners and the role they will play in your startup. Explain any agreements that are in place and what impact they may have on the future of the enterprise.

Recruit your Startup Team

No value proposition is good enough to overcome a poor team. The team's importance cannot be overstated and the set of requirements that the team is expected to meet is both broad and deep. For many entrepreneurs, these expectations can seem overwhelming and unrealistic. It is important that the management team remain fully transparent and cooperative with the prospective Angel. Angels will walk away from otherwise attractive deals if they are uncomfortable with the team.

The plan should include brief biographies of each key team member (with detailed bios in the appendix), addressing in particular the qualifications below.

- **Leadership and management skills.** The CEO should be a motivated, passionate and confident leader with prior experience demonstrating the ability to both lead and manage a group of like-minded people. The team should be positive about their leader and demonstrate a good chemistry amongst them. Angels want to back a leader who is proactive and in control of the situation.

- **Balance between subject matter and business expertise.** To the extent possible, sell your team's experience and expertise in the subject matter of the Company. A team that knows its products and customers from prior positions is a large positive with investors. If you and your team know nothing about the business you are proposing, it will be very difficult to generate enthusiasm for you as the leader of a startup. Along with this expertise, the team should demonstrate that it is well rounded in sales, marketing, product development, operations and finance.

- **Prior startup experience.** Successful entrepreneurs are difficult to find and money tends to flow to entrepreneurs with a history of satisfied investors. Show how the team's prior experience in startup increases the odds of success with the current venture.

- **Demonstrate that you are trustworthy.** When taking Angel money, you should expect some level of Angel involvement. Show early that you will be a good partner and steward of the capital invested. Demonstrate through your experiences that your team is coachable, open to influence, provides high quality and transparent communication, and, of course, carries itself with integrity and credibility.

Many startups don't have a full management team in place when raising Angel money. If this is the case, propose a staffing plan and timing that addresses the gaps that will need to be filled as the business matures.

Your startup may already have a corporate board. If so, include brief bios of each board member that has not been previously provided. Corporate boards can play an important role in fundraising with Angels because they give insight into the credibility earned by the team. A prestigious corporate board can have a significant influence on potential investment. If a board does not exist, you should address what your plans are in this area and the timing of those plans. Angels will expect a corporate board that provides sound overall governance.

In addition to a corporate board, most startups put together an advisory board of senior professionals and thought leaders with subject matter expertise to offer guidance and as an endorsement for the value proposition. If you have such a board, make sure it is engaged, active, and willing to promote your cause. Presenting an advisory board in name only is worse than having no advisory board at all.

Design your Business Model

The business model is the description of how the company will be designed to make money. You should begin with a strong and well though out-go-to market strategy.

The go-to-market strategy outlines how the company intends to deliver its winning value proposition and incorporates three basic components.

- The **Marketing Plan** indicates how you intend to make customers aware of your product. What marketing techniques will you use to find customers and encourage them to find you? What do you envision for your branding strategy?

- The **Selling Plan** articulates precisely how you will sell your customer through what channels. Will you hire representatives to approach customers on your behalf or hire a direct sales force? What are the sales channel options?

- The **Distribution Plan** indicates how you will deliver your products. For example, will you sell and supply distributors or sell and supply customers directly or use a hybrid of both alternatives.

The supply plan should specify out how the product will be produced and made available to customers. Sources of supply should be discussed along with total projected supply costs.

The administration plan provides the basic model for running the back office operations.

When designing your business, above all, make sure it has a viable revenue generating business model that investors can quantify and understand. A free or very low-cost offering may be very attractive to customers, but won't impress investors, since the resulting business may not make money. The implications of the decisions you make are huge, defining your brand image, your funding requirements, and your long-term business viability.

So what are the most common revenue models being used by startups today? Let's discuss some of the most common ones, with a few pros and cons or special considerations for each.

The most common model touted by Internet startups today provides the product or service for free, with all expected revenue from ads and critical mass. This is the so-called "Facebook" model. It's great for customers, but we don't recommend it for startups, unless you have deep pockets. If you have real guts, try the Twitter model of no revenue, counting on the critical mass value from millions of customers.

A variation of this model would provide the product for free, but customers pay for services. In this model, the product is given away for free and the customers are charged for installation, customization, training or ancillary services. This is a good model for getting your foot in the door, but be aware that this is basically a services business with the product as a marketing cost.

Another common variation is called the "freemium" model. In this variation on the free model, used by LinkedIn and many other Internet offerings, the basic services are free, but premium services are available for an additional fee. This also requires a huge investment to get to critical mass, and real work to differentiate and sell premium services to users locked-in as free.

Then there is the more traditional cost-based model. In this more conventional product-pricing model, the price is set at two to five times the product cost. If your product is a commodity, the margin may be as thin as ten percent. Use it when your new technology gives you a tremendous cost improvement. Skip it where there are many competitors.

An alternative is value-based pricing. If you can quantify a large value or cost savings to the customer, charge a price commensurate with the value delivered. This doesn't work well with "nice to have" offerings, like social networks, but does work for new drugs that solve critical health problems.

If you have multiple products, you should consider portfolio pricing. This model is relevant only if you have multiple products and services, each with a different cost and utility.

Here your objective is to make money with the portfolio, some with high markups and some with low, depending on competition, lock-in, value delivered, and loyal customers. This one takes expert management to work.

If you anticipate small customers, as well as very large customers, you will probably need tiered or volume pricing. In certain product environments, where a given enterprise product may have one user or hundreds of thousands, a common approach is to price by user group ranges, or volume usage ranges. Keep the number of tiers small for manageability. This approach doesn't typically apply to consumer products and services.

In heavily competitive environments, the price has to be competitive, no matter what the cost or volume. This model, called competitive positioning, is often a euphemism for pricing low in certain areas to drive competitors out, and high where competition is low. Competing on price alone is a good way to kill your startup.

If you have a base product with add-on features, you can use feature pricing. This approach works if your product can be sold "bare-bones" for a low price, and price increments added for additional features. It can be a very competitive approach, but the product must be designed and built to provide good utility at many levels. This can be a very costly development, testing, documentation, and support challenge.

Finally, there is razor blade pricing. In this model, like cheap printers with expensive ink cartridges, the base unit is often sold below cost, with the anticipation of ongoing revenue from expensive supplies. This is another model that requires deep pockets to start, so is normally not a good option for startups.

Overall, we're huge fans of the "keep it simple stupid (KISS)" principle – customers are typically wary of complex or artificial pricing. Your challenge is to set the right price to match value perceived by the customer, with a fair return for you. It's not a game show, so don't guess - do your research early with real customers.

Build your Execution Plan

Entrepreneurs frequently leave out or provide an inadequate execution plan. The plan should take the form of a timeline that shows all that has been accomplished and what is left to do over the next 3-5 years, particularly in the commercialization area. What is the critical path to revenues or even breakeven? While this plan does not need to be overly detailed, it should provide clear direction and understanding of what you are trying to accomplish by when and where the major milestones fall.

Model your Financial Plan

The financial plan should match up seamlessly with the business plan. It should include an income statement, balance sheet, and cash flow statement that are footed properly, integrated and consistent. Where appropriate, up to five years of historical financial performance should be summarized and included. Typically, the first year of the financial plan should be modeled by month and years 2-5 should be modeled annually.

A summary of the financial model should be included with the business plan, and detailed financial models attached in the appendix. Assumptions should be supplied to make it easy for the Angel to understand the logic behind the numbers. While soliciting professional help here is usually money well spent, the entrepreneur must understand the financial plan and the assumptions that are behind its construction. A poor financial plan will scare off Angels.

Outline your Capital Strategy

The capital plan should begin with the investment history and a basic capitalization table of investors and amounts. Identify the current financial stakeholders and their relationship to management. The capital plan should then include the five-year plan for raising money. Lay out a case for the requested new investment based upon the next milestone or some other material event. Entrepreneurs often ask for too much money without much thought given to where they will end up when that money is spent.

Because most Angel groups invest less than $1 million, they don't expect to always be the last investors in the Company. They want to know what role their investment will play in increasing overall value, whether they should anticipate a follow on investment, and the likelihood of their ownership interest being diluted before exit.

The requested capital should always include a sources and uses statement. This statement shows how the new money will be used at closing. Investors want to know that their money will be used productively in increasing enterprise value.

Additionally, you should provide a proposed valuation and the supporting rational behind that value. For a new startup with a promising future, the initial Angel investment typically comes with a valuation in the $1-$2 million range.

Finally, this section should include an exit pro-forma where the Angel can see your thinking concerning exit method, timing and value.

Where business plans go wrong

Below are common themes found in business plan disasters.

- **The plan is unreadable**. The grammar is so bad, the sentence construction is so painful, or the document organization is such a mess that the investor puts it down without real consideration. Another twist on this problem is when the entrepreneur offers an outdated business plan for review. If you can't bother to keep your plan current, an investor usually won't bother to consider it for investment. If you can't get this part right, how can you possibly be trusted to build a successful business?

- **The plan is too long.** No investor willingly reads an 83-page business plan. It is not uncommon for an author to fall in love with a paragraph or two and use them again and again throughout a plan. More is not better here. Write a plan that says what you want to convey clearly, succinctly, and stop. The plan should be no more than 25 pages, plus attachments.

- **The value proposition is unconvincing.** Many business plans give too much detail about the product and very little explanation of the value proposition. They offer broad market data showing billions of dollars spent in the category, but offer no insight into the customer. Because entrepreneurs are in love with their product, they often assume the whole world will love it too. They neglect to connect their solution to a customer's painful problem and show convincing validation that their superior value proposition is believable.

- **The business model contains significant gaps.** Business plans often lack thoughtfulness and completeness, which results in large gaps in the plan. This can be seen in many ways, but typically these gaps include missing the revenue model, leaving out functional areas of the business where the entrepreneur has no experience, and in particular, not clearly explaining the go-to-market strategy. It is very difficult to evaluate the merits of a startup plan when significant elements are missing.

- **The financial model is incomplete, incompetent or unbelievable.** Very few business plans contain a complete and well thought out set of integrated and accurate financial plans. By accurate, we don't mean that the projections are accurate, just that the math foots correctly and the income statement, balance sheet and cash flow statements are all based on the same set of consistent assumptions. Most entrepreneurs don't have adequate accounting skills to develop financial models without professional help.

- **The valuation is unrealistic.** Most business plans are missing the valuation completely and those that contain a valuation rarely include the rationale for the value. Not offering up a credible valuation and supporting reasoning can easily get a plan thrown out without further consideration.

Chapter 3: Preparing to Meet Your Angel

Execution is all about
Leadership
and **People**

The Entrepreneur's challenge

If you expect to ultimately meet with an Angel, or any other investor, you need to start writing things down early. Many entrepreneurs we meet are not comfortable with their writing skills, so they prefer talking. Talking alone will rarely get you any investors. Investors know that the process of writing things down is part of developing your own full understanding of the venture, and reading it is required by them for a full understanding of your offering and the risks involved.

Thus, a key part of communication for entrepreneurs is business writing. If your business writing needs work, just remember that no one is born with business writing skills, and everyone can learn them. Thus, we include here a quick refresher on business writing basics that might help you more than any business tip toward the next big thing on the horizon:

- **Start with a clear purpose and focus.** Before you start writing, it's important to ask yourself what you intend the document to accomplish. What action you want the reader to take as a result of your message? Make every word focus on that purpose. Get to the point in the first sentence, and restate it in the last.

- **Tailor writing to your audience.** The audience makes all the difference. People subconsciously tailor their conversation, and the same rule applies to writing. Consider your recipient's motivation, culture, socio-economic status, education level, gender, and relationship to you. If you don't know this information, aim high rather than low.

- **Organize toward a specific outcome.** Think about the conclusions you'd like your readers to reach by the time they finish your writing. In general, you will either inform or persuade, and you should have one of these two approaches in mind as you write. Always use the same basic elements of opener, body, and conclusion.

- **Make it look professional.** A poorly formatted document, unsightly fonts, and lack of white space will kill even the best writing. Place all the parts of the message in the correct positions. Use short paragraphs for readability and spacing. Put information where your reader expects to see it. Show your readers respect, and you'll get respect back.

- **Action items should be highlighted and positive.** Underline action items, or even separate them in bullets to give visual cues to their importance. Readers will focus better on positive words rather than negative, so state negative messages in the most positive light to make them more palatable. Focus on what is, rather than what is not.

- **Develop a friendly business writing voice.** This will create a sense of familiarity for investors and customers, making them more open to what you have to say. Inject confidence, and courtesy, always using non-discriminatory language to avoid offence and apparent bias. Write at the audience reading level or below.

In general, we don't recommend phone text-messaging or Instant Messaging for entrepreneur to investor communication, unless the recipient already knows you well. Emails are acceptable, but keep these to one page, addressed to one person, with meaningful subject lines, and use that spell checker.

Always remember that even the best-written message can't convey the body language and emotions of the sender. If the subject is sensitive or the message can be easily misinterpreted, don't use email or anything written, but pick up the telephone or meet in person instead.

Who you are and who you can be, depend on the image your communication brings to the mind of the receiver. That image is set more by the way you communicate, than by the content of your message. For entrepreneurs, skip the story telling and the colorful language, and focus on the message. All parties want to get down to business.

Create an Executive Summary

Modern investors love to first read a two-page summary of your business plan, formatted like a glossy marketing collateral sheet, with text well laid out in columns and sidebars, and a couple of relevant graphics. The goal here is to grab their attention, or they won't look further.

Before you start, remember that the goal of the executive summary is to provide a printed version of your best elevator pitch, to provide a positive first impression to the reader. Think of it as a selling effort, not an attempt to fully describe your startup. Here are the key components of your elevator pitch, and your executive summary:

- **The painful problem and your valuable solution.** These are your hooks, and they better be covered in the first paragraph. State your value proposition, and what specifically you are offering to whom. Skip the acronyms, history of the company, and the disruptive technology behind your solution.

- **Market size and growth opportunity.** Investors are looking for a large and growing market. Spend a few sentences providing the basic market segmentation, size, growth and dynamics - how many people or companies, how many dollars, the buying cycle, how growth rate, and what is driving the segment.

- **Your competitive advantage.** Identify your sustainable competitive advantage, like unique benefits, cost savings, or industry ties. Don't kill your credibility by saying you have no competition. At minimum, you compete with the way things get done currently. Very likely, the investor has already seen multiple plans with similar solutions.

- **Business model.** Who is your customer, what is the price, and how much does it cost you to build one? Do you now have real customers, are just starting development. Outline your sales and marketing strategy (direct marketing, sales channel, viral marketing, and lead generation). Identify key quantities, such as customers, licenses, units, and margin.

- **Executive team.** Remember that investors fund people, more than ideas. Why is your team uniquely qualified to win, and what have they done before? Explain why the background of each team member fits, by naming roles and names of relevant companies. Include outside advisors if they are active and have relevant experience.

- **Financial projections and funding.** You need to show your summary revenue and expense projections for three to five years. Investors need to know the amount of funding you are asking for now, and what they get. The request should generally be the minimum amount of cash you need to reach the next major milestone in your plan.

The above outline need not be applied rigidly or religiously. There is no magic that fits all startups, but make sure you touch on each key issue. You need to think through what points are most important in your particular case, and capitalize on your strengths. Key points skipped become red flags, and investor first impressions will go negative.

A final important element is not even in the executive summary, it is the paragraph you use in the email that introduces your company and has the executive summary attached. Less is more here, so include the grabber, show your passion and commitment, and be sure and ask for something (like a follow-on meeting or specific feedback). That's your metric to see if you have their attention.

Every document and presentation needs to start with an "elevator pitch." An elevator pitch is a concise, well-practiced description of your startup and your plan, delivered with conviction and enthusiasm that your mother should be able to understand, in the time it would take to ride up an elevator. The elevator pitch should be the first few paragraphs of your business plan, your executive summary, your investor presentation, and the first page of your web site.

Understand the Investment Thesis

To be successful with Angels, you need to fully understand the beliefs that Angel investors use when determining what investments to purchase or sell, when to take an action and why. Their investment thesis is what they use to establish goals for their investments, and measures whether they have been achieved.

The most basic investment thesis is to set a target return, such as 10 times the initial investment, and build a diversified portfolio to mitigate the risk. You need to convince investors that investing in your startup will meet their return requirements, with a manageable risk, to be profitable in the long-term for both you and them.

While most Angel investors are investing first and foremost for financial returns, almost all have a secondary goal of helping entrepreneurs succeed through their advice and connections. Some want also to create entrepreneurial wealth in their geographies, because they know that successful entrepreneurs will re-invest some or even most of their winnings in other entrepreneurial ventures. For many of these, the relationship is very important, so make sure you are honest and convincing in building the relationship.

Another element of an Angel's investment thesis that you need to understand is whether a given investor wants to invest alone or with an Angel fund or Angel group. Groups and funds invest in specific types of companies and create due diligence materials on their targets that will almost certainly be different. Some Angels may decide to "go it alone" because they have knowledge about a specific company or industry that Angel groups and funds generally avoid.

Investors always have a reason for investing in each of their ventures. Some are focused on the quality of the management team. Others have to completely understand the idea behind the company in order to invest in it, or look for companies whose product or service they would use themselves. These criteria are not mutually exclusive, but it would serve you well as an entrepreneur to understand as well as possible the driving forces behind every potential investor.

Most investors are only interested in ideas that solve significant problems and are not aimed at merely improving levels of frivolous entertainment. They studiously avoid investing in any idea that would not make them proud to read the headlines as a supporter (e.g. the usual "sin" ideas involving gambling or gaming). It's very frustrating for an entrepreneur when an Angel declines to invest after many hours of involvement due to industry concerns or other factors, which could have been known in the initial meeting.

Another key question that addresses the investment thesis is "How much money should I ask for?" The simple answer is the absolute minimum amount you need to make your plan work. Some entrepreneurs try to start with a huge number, hoping they can negotiate and close on a smaller one, while others understate their requirements, in hopes of getting their foot in the door with an investor.

Neither of these strategies is a good one, as both are likely to damage your credibility with potential investors, even before they look hard at your plan.   Here are the parameters you should use in sizing your request, and be able to explain in justifying your request to investors:

- **Consider implied ownership cost.** If your company is early stage and has a valuation under $1 million, don't ask for a $5 million investment. The investor would be buying your company five times over, and he doesn't want it. If your valuation is around $1 million, you can validly ask for $200-$300 thousand, and offer 20%-30% of your company in exchange.

- **Type of investor.**   Angel investment groups usually won't consider a request over $1 million, while venture capitalists won't look at anything under $2 million. Amounts of $100 thousand or less, are usually relegated to "friends and family."

Approaching any one of these groups with a funding request outside their range is a waste of your time and theirs.

- **Company stage.** If your company is still in the "idea" stage, you have no valuation, so size your investment request on the basis of "goodwill" that you have with your rich uncle, and your business track record. Angels might be interested during "early stage" if you have a prototype, but VCs won't bite until you have a product, customers, and revenue.

- **Calculate what you need, and add a buffer.** Do your financial model first with the volume, cost, and pricing parameters you want. See where your cash flow bottoms out. If it bottoms out at minus $400 thousand, add a 25% buffer, and ask for $500 thousand funding. The request size must tie into your financials to be credible.

- **Investment terms.** The most common case is an equity investment, but there are many terms that can impact what request size is credible. I'm talking about things like anti-dilution clauses, preferred versus common stock, valuation tied to later round, warrants, and bridge loan options. More restrictive terms reduce the credible investment amount.

- **Single or staged delivery.** In many cases, a single investment request may be scheduled for delivery in stages, or tranches (often misspelled as *traunchs* or *traunches*), based on milestone achievement. Obviously, this reduces investor risk and allows a larger commitment, since they can limit their loss if you fail to meet key objectives.

- **Use of funds.** Investors expect to see a "use of funds" list, and they expect the uses to apply only to your core mission. In other words, don't tell investors that you intend to buy a fancy office building or executive cars or pay off prior family member investments with your funding. Even executive salaries should be minimal at this stage.

- **Projected return on investment.** Most entrepreneurs skip this step, but it helps your credibility to include it. Estimate a return on investment (ROI) by projecting company valuation at exit, to show the investor who has 20% what he will get back for that initial investment. He's looking for a 10x return, since he assumes only one in ten survive.

Obviously, determining the proper size of your investment request is a non-trivial exercise, but it's one of the most critical factors for investors in making a decision to invest or not to invest in your company. You need to get it defensibly right the first time, because changing your request under pressure definitely will kill your credibility.

Hone your Investor Presentation

As members of local Angel group selection committees, we've seen a lot of startup presentations to investors, and we've never seen one that was too short - maybe short on content, but not short on pages! A perfect round number is ten slides, with the right content, that can be covered in ten minutes. Even if you have an hour booked, the advice is the same.

Remember the goal is to give an overview presentation that will pique investor interest enough to ask for the business plan and a follow-on meeting, not close the deal on the spot. If you can't get the message across in ten minutes, more time and more charts won't help.

Every startup needs both a business plan and an investor presentation completed before you formally approach any investors. Here are the key slides you need:

- **Problem and market need.** Give the "elevator pitch" for your startup. Explain in analogies your mother could understand, and quantify the "cost-of-pain" in dollars or time. Fuzzy terms like "not user-oriented" or "too expensive" are not helpful.

- **Solution product and technology.** Here is how and why it works, including a customer-centric quantification of the benefits. Make sure to communicate the relevance of your product / services to customer needs. Describe your technology patents and "secret sauce".

- **Opportunity sizing.** Define the characteristics of the overall industry, market forces, market dynamics, and customer landscape. While investors like billion markets with double-digit growth rates, your revenue projections need to be credible. It helps to have data from industry experts like Forrester or Gartner for credibility.

- **Business model.** Explain how you will make money and who pays you (real customers). In this section, you need to be passionate about recurring revenue, profit margin, and volume growth. Implicit in this is the go-to-market strategy.

- **Competition and sustainable advantage.** List and position your competition, or alternatives available to the customer. Highlight your sustainable competitive advantages, and barriers to entry.

- **Marketing, sales, and partners.** Describe your marketing strategy, sales plan, licensing, and partnership plans. Here is also a good place for a rollout timeline with key milestones. Make sure your marketing budget matches the scope of your plan.

- **Executive team.** Qualifications and roles of the top three executives and top three on your Board of Advisors. They need domain knowledge and startup experience. Highlight their level of involvement, and quantify their skin in the game.

- **Financial projections.** Project both revenues and expense totals for next five years, and past three years. What is the current valuation of the company? Show the breakeven point, burn rate, and growth assumptions.

- **Funding requirements and use of funds.** What is the level of capital funding sought during this stage? What equity is the company willing to give in return for the investment? Show a breakdown of the intended uses of these funds.

- **Exit strategy.** What is the planned exit strategy (IPO, merger, sale, including likely candidates), timeframe and return on investment?

Hand out copies of the slides before the presentation for note taking, with proper cover sheet, with brochures, product samples, or other marketing material you may have. Offer to do a demo later, but don't try to squeeze it into the presentation.

Our last recommendation is practice, practice, and practice. The CEO should give the pitch, and prepare by playing "presidential debates" -

asking your team to be the opponents, and check you on timing. Investors really hate long rambling presentations. Show some energy and enthusiasm, and remember if you lose their attention, you have lost the deal.

Also understand that pitch content is only half the story. The other half is how you deliver the message. You need to be energetic and you need to diligently stay on point and on time.

First, make sure you match your material to the time allotted. If you have ten minutes, that means no more than ten slides. Then match your pace to cover all the material. We've seen several presentations that never moved past the first slide before running out of time. An obvious effort to keep talking after the time limit won't save your day with investors.

Remember you are pitching to investors, not customers. Some entrepreneurs seem to think that their product pitch is also their investor pitch. A product pitch is outward focused, on the features and value to a customer, whereas an investor pitch is inward focused, on the business model, costs, ROI, and payback to the investor.

Don't forget to get there in time to check the setup and set the stage. If the projector doesn't work, or won't connect to your laptop, you are the one that loses. Have at least one backup plan, such as copies of your slides to hand out and discuss, in case all else fails. The first words out of your mouth should be "Can everyone hear me and read the screen?"

Also, don't forget to research your audience before presenting. The most respected presenters are the ones who have done the research before hand to know who is in the audience, and have tailored their message to these interests. If you know only a few people in the audience, acknowledge them, and convince the others that this is not a random cold call for you.

Remember that you and your image are key to success, so dress appropriately and professionally. It's always better to be over-dressed than under-dressed. Business casual is the standard. Remember that most investors are from a generation where faded and torn jeans were on the wrong side of success in business.

Let the top person do the talking. Tag team shows don't work in short time frames. More importantly, investors want to see and hear the top guy – typically the Founder or CEO. They will be judging his clarity, aptitude, character, and passion. Others can be present for effect, but deferrals to team members for answers are a sign of weakness.

On all key points, lead with facts, and skip the background details. Skip the generic marketing phrases like more user friendly, massive opportunity, and paradigm shifting. "According to Gartner, the opportunity is 100 million by 2015, with 12% compounded growth." Investors don't need to know the implementation details of your patent or customer support plan.

Finally, don't forget to ask for the order. How much money do you need, and what percent of your company are you willing give up for that amount? If you want investor interest, the business parameters of a deal should be presented as clearly as the product parameters.

Close by asking for questions and promising follow-up. Acknowledging feedback and actually listening for ways to improve will always lead to a positive impression. You should answer questions with data if you have it, but avoid defensive responses in favor of a promise to follow-up after the meeting.

Forget the theory that you can "rise to the occasion" and impress everyone with your dynamic speaking ability. If you are pitching the wrong point in the wrong way, the occasion will be more the demise than the rise of your dream.

Where Angel introductions go wrong

Angel introductions can go wrong for many reasons, but the most common one is engaging an Angel too early. "Too early" means you have a startup idea, but you haven't yet developed it into an investable business. The result is that both you and the investor are frustrated with the discussion, and you have probably lost that once chance to make a good first impression. The relationship and potential interest from both sides is probably dead.

In fact, we're sure you realize that there is quite a distance between a great idea and a great company. But many people don't have a clue on how to bridge the gap. So, here are some thoughts on due diligence of any idea before spending your time and money, or presenting it to any investor. Make sure you look hard at your idea as a business, and make sure it has the following positives:

- **Competitors are few.** Use Google or one of the many other search engines to search for existing solutions to this problem. A search argument like "recipes from the ingredients you have on hand" might be the place to start. If you find ten competitors who already have this offering, it's probably not worth going any further.

- **No known patents filed.** Maybe the solution hasn't yet been commercialized, but if someone else has submitted a patent, it puts your idea in jeopardy. If so, another series of searches on Google Patents and the US Patent Office site and Free Patents Online is in order at this point. Of course, you could pay a Patent Attorney a few thousand dollars to do a professional search.

- **Large and growing market.** Investors will expect market analysis data from a "credible unbiased third party" – that means a nationally known market research firm like Gartner, Forrester, IDC, or many others. Hopefully, you will find, with your favorite search engine, something like the "Cooking Sauces & Food Seasonings Market Report 2012."

- **Real customer pain and money.** Your own conviction that if you love the product, everyone will love the product, doesn't count. Customers may "like" a product, but will generally only pay for things they "need," physically or emotionally. Talk to experts in this domain (chefs, home cooking fanatics), and listen for hidden requirements and challenges.

- **Whole solution viability.** Many products fail because of "dependencies" and hidden costs. Auto engines that burn hydrogen are "easy," but getting service stations built around the world and new safety legislation takes decades. Make sure you understand all costs, interdependencies, sales channels, marketing requirements, and cultural issues.

- **Motivated and qualified team is ready.** The most critical step is to decide if you really have the passion, experience, and team for creating this solution into a business. Startups are tough on even the most dedicated and passionate Founders – others will likely fail, and definitely be unhappy. No idea is worth that.

Another sensitive point between some entrepreneurs and Angel investors is the fact that some groups of Angel investors charge entrepreneurs a fee to pitch to their groups. This practice has caused a rousing debate among key players, with some calling it a scam, and others defending it as necessary to cover expenses.

Some people attack this practice on ethical grounds, and call out popular Angel groups which charge fees ranging from several hundred dollars to $5,000 or more as scams, or "Angel group" payola. Others have spoken out in defense of the practice, at least for smaller amounts, commenting that, aside from covering expenses, it also provides a degree of "filtering". In reality, these fees are usually trivial compared to the real costs of preparing, travelling, and presenting to investors.

While we're definitely proponents of full disclosure to prevent surprises, we see nothing wrong with experienced investors charging a fee for listening and evaluating startup proposals, and providing feedback (or funding) to entrepreneurs to help them achieve their objectives. Lawyers and other professional consultants have done this for generations.

We have long recommended that entrepreneurs do their own "due diligence" on potential investors and Angel groups before they waste their time and hard-strapped funds, and here are some additional thoughts for entrepreneurs thinking of paying to pitch their case to investors:

- **Be realistic about expectations of funding success.** According to the latest data from Gust, only about 3 out of 100 companies who initiate the formal funding request to Angel groups actually get funded. Entrepreneurs who expect to get a hit the first time (or first five times) they pitch their story cold are likely to be disappointed.

- **Improve your odds by networking and warm introductions first.** With the rise of social tools, potential investors are increasingly more accessible outside the pitch room. If they know you by a warm introduction from a friend well before the pitch, or you have one or more advocates in the room, your odds of success go up dramatically.

- **Evaluate feedback from individual investors first.** If you have been given private introductions, but the investors declined to hear your pitch, don't assume that paying money or presenting to larger numbers will solve your problem. There is probably a fundamental problem with your business or how you present it. Find and fix that first.

- **Weigh the cost against the track record and "reach" of a specific Angel group.** A fair question to ask any Angel group, fee or no fee, is "What is your track record of funded investments, versus number of pitches?" Spending $1 thousand to get $1 million is usually better than spending nothing to get nothing. Does their "sweet spot" match your type of business?

- **Consider your startup stage.** If you're in seed-stage with young, first-time Founders, and think you're ready to raise some capital, your odds of funding success are so low that we would skip the fee alternatives. On the other hand, if you have solid revenues, good growth, and need to scale faster, it may be worthwhile to get to the best Angels in town.

- **Don't wait until you are desperate.** Investors can spot an out-of-money entrepreneur a mile away. They won't even notice that you are angry because you had to pay for the opportunity, and they won't fund you on principle, since it doesn't appear that you can manage your plan very well.

Remember that Angels are always looking for better ways to make use of their time, and quickly find the entrepreneurs who have the best case and the least risk. They make money from win-win situations and it's up to you to take the right first step.

Chapter 4: Getting Angel Funding

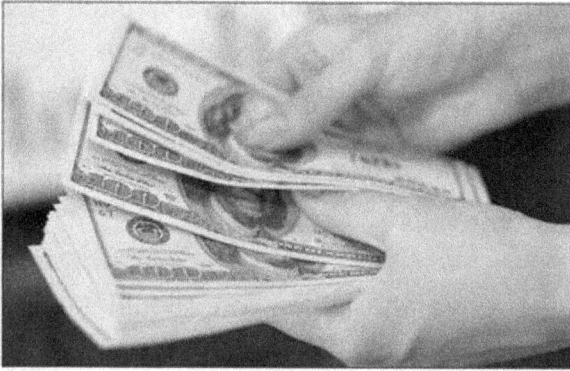

Funding Your Business is an
Endless Quest

The Angel Group Investment Process

Step 1: Pre-Screening

The first question to be answered is "Should our group bother to consider this opportunity?"

The Angel evaluation usually begins with a pre-screening step, where new opportunities are vetted. The introduction should begin with the submission of the executive summary and the investment thesis. Angel groups typically have a fund manager or managing partner who accepts and evaluates initial submissions. Sometimes, not always, you will have the opportunity to give your elevator pitch to this person. Because most Angel groups see over 100 deals a year, it is easy to get rejected quickly without serious consideration. You must give the Angel a reason to keep your opportunity alive.

To the extent possible, you should begin by obtaining whatever information you can find concerning the deal criteria used by the Angel group you are approaching. To save time and effort, most Angel groups make their criteria available, usually on their website. At this stage the Angel group is looking for basic information.

- Are the documents readable?
- Is the opportunity credible?
- Is the opportunity within our geographic region?
- Is the amount of money requested in our range?
- Does this industry or stage of company interest us?
- Are the basic deal terms worth discussing further?

Sometimes an Angel group will require that the opportunity be entered into Gust, the Angel community software package used to manage deal flow This process requires more complete information than just an executive summary or investment thesis. Either way, most Angels will not read a full business plan until the company has survived early vetting. There are simply too many competing opportunities for an Angel to consider spending any meaningful time studying a business plan this early.

You should not expect an Angel group to sign a non-disclosure agreement (NDA) at this stage. Enforcing such a pledge is practically impossible with a group's membership, so the standard industry practice is not to consider an NDA until a term sheet is signed, a group of interested investors has been identified, and serious due diligence is ready to begin. Do not share anything you consider proprietary information, such as formulas, trade secrets, etc. in your business plan. Business and financial plan information is generally not considered confidential in a startup business looking for investment capital.

A typical outcome of the pre-screening step is that maybe 10-20% of the opportunities submitted move onto Screening Committee consideration.

Step 2: The Screening Committee

The Screening Committee has to answer the question "Does the opportunity look promising?"

It is typically comprised of six to ten seasoned Angels who volunteer their time to filter and select companies to present to the larger membership. They usually meet 2-4 weeks prior to a member meeting and consider three to six opportunities to be whittled down to two or three companies for member meeting presentations.

If you pass the pre-screening step, you will be invited to make a ten to fifteen minute presentation to the Screening Committee, followed by fifteen to twenty minutes of questions by committee members. If the company is selected to present to the member meeting, a Screening Committee member will typically follow up with the company. This person will read and study the business plan, ask more detailed questions, prepare a preliminary due diligence report assessing the opportunity for the larger membership, and later present that report to the members. This person can have great influence over the members' perception of the opportunity's appeal.

Step 3: Member Meeting Presentation

Opportunities that get the support of the Screening Committee are invited to present to the full Angel group. The real test here is whether the members like the opportunity.

Angel groups vary in their member meeting frequency from as often as monthly to as little as quarterly or even less. Some groups only meet as attractive opportunities present themselves. The group size can be as few as a half dozen to over one hundred attendees. Some meetings are restricted to paid members only, while others invite anyone who professes to be an accredited investor, along with many guests and service providers such as accountants, advertising agencies and attorneys. Meeting formats can be focused only on business, where two or three opportunities are presented, or they can be very social, including a meal and drinks, educational presentations, a couple of investment opportunities, plus a reception for networking. Because of this variety, you should assume that any information shared in an Angel member meeting is broadly shared outside the meeting.

The most common member meeting format is to have the company CEO present a 15-minute overview summarizing the opportunity, followed by 15 minutes of questions from the audience. Company representatives are then asked to leave and the preliminary due diligence report is presented by one of the group's members, usually a selection committee member.

The member meeting usually represents the company's one opportunity to gain broad interest and support toward an investment from the group. An attendance and presentation do-over is generally not allowed at this stage. In roughly fifteen minutes, you must minimally convey the winning value proposition, the large revenue potential, the impressive management team and a plan that convinces the listener that an investment in your opportunity will be satisfying and successful.

Step 4: Assessing Investment Interest

The goal of this step is to negotiate a win-win deal between one or more Angel investors and the entrepreneur.

Once the member meeting has been completed, the Angel group leader will poll each of the group's members for their interest in the deal and at what level of investment. The goal will be to round up enough member interest to go forward with a term sheet and due diligence. It usually takes a week or two to know if a deal has enough momentum to go forward. The median Angel group investment is about $700,000, with the typical individual Angel investing about $25,000 to $100,000. Most Angel groups will not go forward with a membership interest of less than a $100,000 total investment.

Step 5: Term Sheet Agreement

A term sheet is a non-binding agreement between a Corporation and an investor that outlines the major terms under which an investment is contemplated. Negotiating a term sheet is arguably the most difficult step in the Angel investment process. It is here that the entrepreneur is introduced to a world of terms and concepts that are confusing and difficult to understand. By this time, you should have engaged an attorney who understands Angel investment terminology, will guide you through the negotiation process, and can craft a win-win deal.

Step 6: Due Diligence

Due diligence typically occurs once a term sheet has been signed. The purpose of due diligence for the Angel group is twofold; first to confirm the claims, assumptions, and intentions made by the company and, second, to fill-in missing information and knowledge gaps. The result of good due diligence is a thorough analysis of the opportunity, an assessment of the risk/reward relationship of the investment and a recommended action on the opportunity.

An Angel group will usually identify a due diligence team of 3-5 investors with a team member named as the lead. The team may or may not receive compensation from the Angel group to perform its duties. Due diligence is a process that can take anywhere from 30 to 90 days, depending upon the complexity of the situation being studied and the amount of investment involved. The company should be as proactive and helpful as possible. A good and positive due diligence process provides the basis for a longer-term transparent and productive working relationship between management and investors. A standard due diligence process reviews the following areas.

- **Management team and owners.** Expect interviews and background checks for each key team member and most owners. Be proactive in revealing your self and your team. If there are issues needing to be explained, such as a past bankruptcy or a lawsuit, it is better to inform the due diligence team up front, rather than have the issue come up as a negative surprise later.

- **Market and competition.** This usually requires independent confirmation and assessment of the target market size and quality. This is the traditional market research, where third party information is used to challenge management's claims of the total revenue opportunity and the company's addressable share of the market. The due diligence team will also seek to better understand the competition through publicly available information, networks and contacts. The team will study the revenue size of the competition and the present go-to-market strategies for competing solutions.

- **Business Model.** The company's business model is assessed for its viability relative to competitive business models and to other potential business model options. This is accomplished through interviews, the study of competitors and the experience of the Angels and their network.

- **Products/Services.** An Angel group will often call upon a product or technology specialist to provide a technical assessment and opinion on the commercial application of the company's product. The specialist will usually assess the quality of the product's intended function as well as the development plan that supports the commercialization of the product.

- **Legal.** If they haven't already done so, the Angel group will involve an attorney beginning with the due diligence process to evaluate the corporation's governance history for any legal challenges or red flags affecting the company's investment attractiveness. The Angel group will thoroughly review all incorporation work, contracts, beneficial relationships, employment agreements, and obligations of the company. It is not unusual for an otherwise good company to be virtually un-investable due to prior corporate formation and governance mistakes.

- **Financial.** Financial due diligence can be very simple or very involved depending upon the stage of the company, the level of investment, and the capital structure. The team will study in detail the internal financial statements and prior tax returns, evaluate the company's CFO capabilities, and talk to the company's accountants and financial advisors. The team will require a pre-investment and post-investment capitalization table, clearly laying out all financial stakeholders in the entity.

- **Intellectual Property.** An intellectual property review will focus on the open status of all filings, granted patents and ownership status. Generally, Angels will not invest in a company where the founder holds the company's patent in a related entity. Investors see patents being held in a different entity as a sign of bad faith by a company's ownership.

At the satisfactory conclusion of due diligence, the team creates a due diligence report that analyzes the pros and cons of the investment, the additional steps that need to be taken and a recommendation of whether or not to go forward with the investment. This report is typically shared with those members who are interested in the deal at a due diligence report back meeting. A positive due diligence experience will often increase momentum for a deal and bring in new money from the larger group.

Step 7: Deal Closing

Closing a deal occurs very rarely relative to the total deals seen by the Angel group. Most Angel groups will invest in 2 to 5% of the total deals they see in a year. From initial introduction to closing, the entrepreneur should expect a total timeline of three to six months. It can take quite a while for an Angel group to round up its members, answer questions, and get paperwork and checks signed and mailed for closing. It is common for the company to pay for the deal fees of the investment, while the Angel group's attorney usually prepares the deal paperwork.

The Angel Group Evaluation

While there is an infinite number of ways Angel groups may consider a potential investment, there are consistent assessment elements that each will use for opportunity evaluation. We have organized this assessment and decision making process as a series of eight modules. Each module builds on top of the foundation created by the previous module, as the Angel group works through the information gathering and decision processing necessary to get satisfactory answers to the critical investment questions.

Proposition - Is the big idea a winner?

First and foremost, the group wants to back a value proposition that is a clear winner. Ideally this will include a well-defined target customer, a painful problem that is not adequately being solved, a convincing solution that solves the problem better than all others, and a substantial benefit that the customer highly values.

Where possible, the value proposition's claims include convincing evidence with customer examples that support the case. You want to illustrate why your solution is best and what sustainable competitive advantage you will have in the marketplace. Here you want to offer any intellectual property or trade secrets that will contribute to your competitive advantage. You also want to address the hurdles that must be overcome for the value proposition to be commercially successfully.

Investors will want satisfactory answers to the following questions.

- Who is the target customer and what is the quality of this customer?
- How do you know the customer has a big and painful problem?

- Why is their problem not being solved already?
- How will your company uniquely solve this problem?
- What benefit will the customer see in your solution?
- What evidence do you have to support your claims?
- What is the current customer experience with your solution?
- How large is the competitive threat to your solution?

The large majority of startup entrepreneurs do not do an adequate job of defining and defending their value proposition. What is self evident to the entrepreneur is rarely convincing to the customer or the investor. You cannot put too much effort into defining your value proposition and providing believable, customer-based evidence that your claims are true.

Potential – Are revenues big enough?

Having built the case for a strong value proposition, Angels need to be convinced that there is a large revenue opportunity available by delivering that value proposition. This revenue estimate should as specific as possible, very pragmatically generated and sensible to defend.

Investors will want satisfactory answers to the following questions.

- What geography will you be addressing?
- How many target customers exist?
- What products will you sell your customer - how many, for what price and how often?
- Based upon these assumptions, what is your total annual revenue opportunity?
- What competitors currently have what percentage of market share?
- What share of this market do you estimate you will capture within five years? Are these revenue projections credible?
- What are the pricing assumptions relative to your competition?
- What are the global trends moving both in favor of your solution, as well as against it?

Angels need to know that an opportunity's revenues will be big enough to provide a high rate of return within five years. A good idea that generates planned sales of $5 million within five years will not attract any interest. Planned revenues need to be a very minimum of $20 million within five years of startup.

People - Is the team right for the job?

Angels want to invest in winners, especially a team that has a demonstrated track record of past successes in similar situations. Because those teams are hard to find, Angels often must evaluate a team against some ideal model. In building your management team, you want a mix of industry and functional experience, along with a strong CEO leader who can sell the vision. Where your team is short of the desired members, you should lay out your plan to acquire them and specifically identify them where possible.

Angels desire a management team that ideally demonstrates the following characteristics:

- Intention - Is the team completely invested in this opportunity?
- Industry knowledge - Does the team know the industry and is it close to the target customer?
- Expertise - Does the team have the skills in sales, marketing, product development, finance, and operations to execute the opportunity?
- Chemistry - Does the team get along, complement each other, and work well together?

- Coachable – Can the team be influenced and will it accept advisors, investors, and partners?
- Trustworthy - Does the team demonstrate the honesty and integrity necessary to be a responsible steward of the Angels' investment?

Plan – Can it become a Company?

It's not enough that the value proposition is a big winner; you must also demonstrate that you can design and execute a business model and plan that will successfully deliver that value proposition to your target customer. The business model design is your opportunity to convince the investor that you know who the customer is, how to reach that customer, close the sale, and supply product that the customer values highly. The Angel group will want to know a bit of company history, what the company has accomplished versus its business plan so far, the business plan intentions going forward, and the immediate execution plans for the next six months to one year.

Investors will want satisfactory answers to the following questions.

- Is there a competitive opening for this business?

- How will the Company develop, test and rollout its product strategy?
- How will the Company generate demand for its product?
- How will the Company go-to-market?
- How will the Company supply its product?
- How will the Company manage customer relationships?

Profit - Can it make money?

Most startup opportunities fall way short when presenting the financial plan that supports the business plan. A credible financial plan is an absolute necessity to getting Angel group funding. The financial plan should cover a five-year time horizon, include an integrated income statement, balance sheet, and cash flow statement and show major assumptions.

Investors will want satisfactory answers to the following questions.

- How will the business make money?
- Is the financial plan credible?
- Are the cost drivers and cost structure credible?
- Are the gross margins attractive?
- Are the working capital requirements acceptable?

- How much cash will it take to get to break even and by when?

Price – Is the investment attractive?

When evaluating an investment opportunity, Angels will assess the opportunity's pre-money valuation, which is the value of the enterprise immediately prior to investment. It is very common for entrepreneurs to bring opportunities to Angels without serious consideration given to the value of the enterprise and the rationale behind that value. This situation often occurs because of an unrealistic expectation from the entrepreneur for both the requested amount of money and the ownership offer to the investor in return for that money.

When a good sense of value does not exist, the investment negotiations can be difficult and frustrating. An unrealistically high pre-money valuation can be a non-starter for investment negotiations. Most Angel group investments are made in the range of $500,000 to $1,000,000 at a value of about $1 to $2.5 million pre-money for an ownership percent in the range of 10-40%.

Terms. Generally speaking, Angels want deal terms that provide some preferential treatment for their investment risk relative to management and friends and family already invested in the company. The deal terms for any Angel investment fall into the following main categories.

Equity type. The form of the corporation can have a significant impact on investor interest. You should have an attorney involved in incorporating your firm, as different corporate forms have different taxability and investment implications. Generally, pass-through entities such as LLC's and S corporations are useful if no further investment beyond Angel money is contemplated. If VC money is envisioned, then a C corp. form is the preferred choice. Convertible debt is used when a valuation is difficult to agree upon and the parties desire to punt that decision to further rounds of investment down the road.

Investment and funding intention. The provision defines the amount of money to be invested and the percentage of ownership to be acquired for that investment. If the investment will be made in tranches, that will also be defined here.

Corporate governance. This will include the Board of Directors composition and the definition of the Directors and Officers insurance to be supplied by the company for the Directors protection. Depending on the size of the investment, Angel groups frequently desire to have one or more board seats.

Investor rights. It is common for Angels to require preferred shares of the company with their investment that give them a certain sets of preferential rights. These rights can also come in the form of a separate side agreement along with a common shares purchase.

Information Rights. The investors will desire access to certain information such as business plans, budgets, financial statements, annual audits, and management reports.

Dividends. These are proceeds paid by a company to its shareholders. There are generally approved and paid in accordance with procedures worked out in the term sheet. In a startup, it is common to accrue unpaid dividends rather than return cash to investors. Dividends are often used in preferred stock to protect some minimum rate of return for the investor group.

Voting rights. These are the rights afforded the investment group relative to major corporate decisions, such as a sale or change of control. It may also provide for a single voice to represent the 10-30 individual investors in the deal.

Anti dilution. This provision preserves of the groups' percentage ownership in the company without being forced to make a new investment. It gives the group protection against future investment at a lower valuation.

Right of first refusal. Gives the group the right to participate in future investment rounds.

Registration. Allows the investor group to sell their stock if the company participates in an Initial Public Offering (IPO).

Redemption. Provides a procedure for the investor group to exit at a predetermined price without an IPO or sale of the company. This provision gives the investor group the ability to get out of the deal with an acceptable return in a timeframe of their choosing.

Liquidation preference. Upon a liquidity event, this provides a preference to the Angel group for the cash disbursement over founders and previous investors. It provides a layer of protection for the investors that their return of capital is first in line to be paid. There are a variety of procedures used here with varying degrees of advantage accruing to the investor group.

Due diligence. Due diligence is the examination of the company and its stakeholders to validate the investment's desirability. Terms sheets have a due diligence contingency clause allowing the investor to walk away from the deal if they find conditions unsatisfactory after further study.

Expenses. The company generally pays deal expenses. Sometimes an investor group will also request a due diligence fee.

Overall Funding Strategy. Angels want to see the overall funding strategy of the company. Most companies will require several funding rounds. In addition to the investment being contemplated, the investor group will want to see a longer term funding plan, maybe five years, which captures the full thinking of the management team. This allows the investor group to evaluate their likelihood of dilution and the need for protection. It also gives the group visibility into the need for further Angel investment down the road. Angels commonly hold some money back for the next round of investment.

It has become much more common for Angel groups to invest in smaller milestone-based achievements rather than open-ended larger investments. If ever there were any, the days of obtaining a couple of million dollars without a specific milestone and spending plan are over. Angel groups want to know that their investment will move the company forward to a next funding step that increases the company's valuation.

Relative to the investment itself, investors will want satisfactory answers to the following questions.

- How much money is being requested at what valuation?
- Are the terms favorable to the investor group?
- Is the investment requested enough to reach a meaningful milestone?
- How does this investment fit into the overall funding strategy?
- What are the sources and uses?

- Has the company made good progress with their current resources?
- Will the next milestone create significant value for the business?
- What is the planned exit timing and return?

Participation – Can we work together?

Angels want to invest in people that they like and trust and can positively influence. Because Angels contribute time and talent and money to an investment, they want to understand going into the deal how the parties will work together. This begins with a review of the corporation's governance practices.

A corporation's governance system is comprised of its policies, procedures, and accountability that is meant to ensure that the company delivers fair and ethical treatment for all of its stakeholders and that it provides a fair resolution of conflicts among them. The corporate governance responsibility typically sits with the Board of Directors. Angels want to see a corporate governance structure that exhibits transparency, integrity and a willingness to be influenced by a new stakeholder.

If you haven't already done so, you should expect to constitute a new board of directors with your new Angel group investment. Typically, boards are comprised of three to seven members. The board composition will be negotiated prior to an Angel group investment. The group usually wants at least a single board member to represent and protect the Angel group's interest. It is common to have a five-person board, two chosen by the founder, two chosen by the Angel group, and one outsider agreed-to by both groups. Board meetings are typically held monthly and last two to four hours each. You should plan to pay board members some compensation for their involvement. This can come in the form of cash, stock options, or a hybrid, but we strongly recommend some form of compensation for the Angel representative. This is typically agreed-to through the term sheet.

Relative to participation, investors will want satisfactory answers to the following questions.

- What's the governance plan?
- What will the Angel group's involvement be?
- What is the next milestone plan?
- How will we monitor progress?

Partnership – Can we exit successfully?

Angel groups typically look for the Angel with the most potential benefit to offer the company to represent its interests. There are many ways Angels contribute to the achievement of a company's success. Consider a few below.

Business wisdom. Angel investors not only contribute money to an opportunity, but also important wisdom acquired from prior experience in areas such as stakeholder relations, employee hiring, and strategic planning. Ultimately, it's this intangible capability that can add the most value to the company.

Emotional maturity. Entrepreneurship is inherently full of mood swings. An Angel investor can be a great coach and mentor, sometimes providing the only shoulder an entrepreneur can cry on during difficult times. Good investor/ entrepreneur relationships often grow informally into regular communications covering a wide range of topics. This mentoring can be particularly useful to the entrepreneur working through the personality issues that tend to dominate start up companies.

Expertise. Along with business wisdom and emotional maturity, the valuable investor will possess specific expertise in the business. Some Angel investors only invest in industries where they have knowledge and prior experience. The more industry experience an investor has, the more useful she can be.

Network. Angel investors typically participate in networks of other Angel investors and venture capital firms that are available for evaluation, feedback and syndication. This access can be extremely valuable to an entrepreneur attempting to find additional funding, hiring key people, or approaching prospective customers.

The Angel group will have negotiated reporting of key company information, typically monthly or quarterly. They may also ask the company CEO to report back to the group annually. There will likely be a set of key metrics that the company will monitor in its regular reports.

You should plan for a successful exit of the company with the initial outside investment. This should be addressed by considering the path to exit, the probable length of time to exit, and the expected value at exit. It is important to know what you are intending to accomplish and set your sights and focus on the end game from the very beginning.

Relative to the post closing monitoring of the investment, investors will want satisfactory answers to the following questions.

- Who's going to monitor this investment?
- How will we build a successful relationship?
- How will we communicate with the team and our members?
- How can we increase the odds of success?
- How can we prepare for exit?

Chapter 5: Final Thoughts

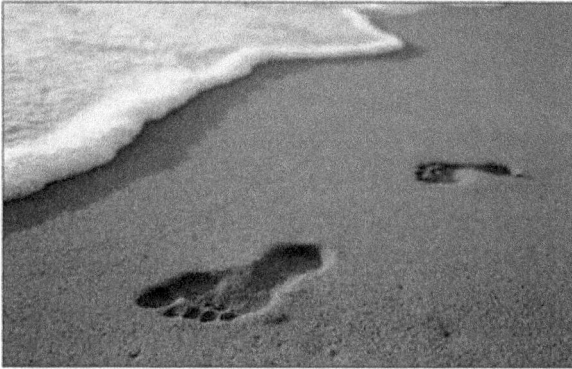

Random **Musings**
and **Prognostications**

What we've learned

Hopefully, what you have learned by now is that Angels are a particularly rare breed of investor, driven by a desire to help, as well as a desire to make big money from some exciting and very risky opportunities.

They always invest their own money, as compared to venture capitalists and private equity investors, who typically invest and manage other people's money in new businesses.

The second lesson we're sure you have all concluded by now is that finding funding is hard work. It takes a lot of time to prepare and do the networking, and the rules change as you move through the various stages of a new business. Angel investors typically provide earlier-stage funding, after friends and family, while venture capital firms typically come in at later stages.

Of course, growth and development are really a continuum. For perspective, here is a summary of how investors of all types will categorize your progress, and where Angels fit:

- **Idea stage.** This is the initial excitement period, the time when you dream of riches and fantasize the life of a business owner, but you have no real plan. At this stage, no professional investor will touch you unless you have a beautiful track record of success with previous startups. Funding will only come from you, or friends, family, and fools.

- **Early or embryonic stage.** Investments at this stage are typically called seed investments. Funding of $250,000-$1 million is available from Angels, if you have credentials and have done the homework of a good business plan, financial model, and executive presentation. Anything less the $250,000, or any amount at this stage with no personal credentials, still has to come from friends and families, loans, or federal grant sources.

- **Funding or rollout stage.** This is the realm of venture capital professional investors, with funding amounts of $1-10 million, often referred to as the "A-round," or first institutional funding. At this stage, your startup better be selling a commercial offering, have price and cost validated, with significant customer sales and a real revenue stream. Lesser amounts of revenue might still put you in the Angel realm.

- **Growth stage.** Additional funding rounds for growth are often called the "B-round" through "G-round," with each being in the $5 million to more than $50 million from venture capital and other sources. Companies at this stage must have a large market, good traction, and be focused on scaling infrastructure and market adoption. This normally means more than 30 employees, and more than $1 million in revenue.

- **Exit stage.** This is the final stage of investment in venture opportunities, and is the point where Angel investors expect to see the return and gain from the original investment. At this stage, you need investment bankers to negotiate a merger or acquisition (M&A), go private, or help you go public with an Initial Public Offering (IPO).

Obviously, if you bootstrap your business, you can ignore all these stages and the investment implications. Otherwise, not paying attention to the expectations associated with each stage will likely jeopardize your chance of landing the big one.

A third lesson is the need for a written business plan, as detailed in Chapter 2, surrounded by the necessary supporting documents, including an Executive Summary, an Investor Presentation, and a Financial Model.

A business plan need not be a large document with impressive graphics. In preparing it, try to look at your project through the investors' eyes. The goal should be to include answers to every question an investor could possibly ask, except maybe "where do I sign"?

Why the odds are long

The odds of landing an Angel investment are still long due to the simple fact that there are many more entrepreneurs looking for funding, than there is money available. In addition, odds are long since the risk is high - statistics say that the failure rate for new businesses within the first 5 years is as high as 90 percent.

Therefore, even though Angel investors in 2010 contributed over $20 billion to 60,000 startups, it's a hard road for both sides. There is so much written these days about how to attract investors that most entrepreneurs "assume" they need funding, and don't even consider a plan for "bootstrapping," or self-financing their startup. Yet, according to many sources, over 90 percent of all businesses are started and grown with no equity financing, and many others would have been better off without it, as too much money can kill a business almost as effectively as not enough.

Why the journey is fun anyway

By definition, entrepreneurs love the art of the start. Assuming your startup takes off, you will probably find that the fun is gone by the time you reach 50 employees, or a few million in revenue. The Founder and CEO job changes from creating a "work of art" to operating a "cookie cutter."

Many people believe that good entrepreneurs are naturally born, rather than trained or experienced in the art of business. We believe there is a natural born component required, but often we tend to agree with Peter Drucker, who said, "It's not magic, it's not mysterious, and it has nothing to do with genes. It's a discipline, and like any discipline, it can be learned."

On the natural born side, good entrepreneurs seem to have a strong vision and the ability to inspirationally lead others. It is this vision that is the beacon to drive the right people behavior, leading to the success of the business. Chances are you chose the entrepreneur lifestyle to attain some level of satisfaction in the first place, so remember; the fun is in the journey, not just the destination.

If you feel you have the vision characteristics, your journey will be more fun if you add some of the key learnable skills that can improve the success and impact of every entrepreneur. Here are some thoughts assembled from an interview with Herb Kelleher of Southwest Airlines and other executives.

Most important is the ability to set priorities and focus on goals. Many people allow themselves to be driven by the crisis of the moment. Personal discipline is the key word here. Set yourself some priorities and goals, and live by them.

Close behind is the ability to identify important issues. Some people call this common sense; others call it "street smarts." In the normal startup environment, there are multiple forces competing for your attention every day, and you need to learn to delegate or ignore many. It relates back to experience and knowledge, more than genes.

Of course, you always have to have the conviction to be a passionate advocate. When you believe in something enough to turn your passion into action, you have become an advocate. That power and voice is then used to persuade others to make the correct decision. An effective advocate requires conviction, usually acquired during related first hand experience or training.

But passion is no substitute for broad knowledge and experience. Experience allows one to tackle challenges with confidence in a given area. Broad knowledge facilitates the same success in other business areas.

Entrepreneurs need this, because their challenges are across the spectrum from technical to legal, operational, financial, and organizational.

The way to gain knowledge is to practice active listening skills. Above all, the ability to listen and understand the real meaning of what people are saying (and not saying) is paramount, because the most important information never arrives in reports or email. Some people pick this up from experience, and others find classroom courses most helpful in setting the focus.

After you listen and evaluate the input, it takes sound judgment to make the right decisions. We don't think anyone is born with sound judgment; it has to be learned, but can be started at a very early age. Every entrepreneur must have the capacity to assess situations or circumstances shrewdly and to draw proper conclusions.

Sound judgment should always be tempered with a pleasant skepticism. Skepticism is not doubting, but applying reason and critical thinking to determine validity. It's the process of searching for a supportable conclusion, as opposed to justifying a preconceived conclusion. It is a learned skill.

These all revolve around the larger theme of team building. In short, to succeed, the entrepreneur must see and articulate a vision in order to attract and motivate a team, then be able to identify the key issues, challenge the views held within the team, and make judgments from among the varying perspectives in the team.

If finding investors is your biggest detriment to fun, you should stick with bootstrapping. This will allow you to retain full control of your business, and you don't have an investor "boss" second-guessing every move, and you don't have to spend months begging for money.

Above all, do what you love, and you will love what you do. It's hard to be successful if you don't enjoy the subject area, the team, the challenge, and the customers. In fact, failure while having fun is not usually seen as life-threatening, and is certainly a learning experience. Expect that some ideas will fail in the process of learning. Rather than treating the mistakes as failures, think of them as fun experiments.

Fun is all about creativity; innovation, play, experimentation, progress, and seeing real things come to life. The most innovative people don't see any dichotomy between work and fun. If all this makes your creative juices flow, it's time to get started, and get positioned for Angel funding. You too can be one of those rare and talented individuals who has been touched by an Angel.

Index

www.ingramcontent.com/pod-product-compliance
Lightning Source LLC
Chambersburg PA
CBHW031501180326
41458CB00044B/6656/J